Remember to adapt the guide to the laws and regulations of your country, as these may vary. Additionally, it is important to keep the information up-to-date, as the real estate market can change over time. Good luck with your guide!

Legal Information

Book Title: Complete Guide for Property Buyers

Author: Dionisio Melo

Publishing Name: Independent Publication

ISBN: 9798877458321

Preface

In the thrilling journey towards property acquisition, it is imperative to acknowledge from the outset that every country, every region, has its own laws and unique ways of approaching the real estate process. This preface serves as an essential reminder of the diversity in the legal and financial landscape you will encounter as you embark on this journey in different parts of the world.

Property acquisition is not merely a transactional act but an immersion into the social, legal, and economic fabric of a specific community. From legal documents to financing processes, each country presents its set of regulations and traditions that are crucial to understand and respect.

In this context, each chapter of this guide is designed to provide universal principles applicable in most cases, while also focusing on offering insights on how to adapt to the peculiarities and singularities of different real estate environments. The information provided is a valuable starting point, but consulting with local professionals is crucial to ensure a comprehensive and accurate understanding of the specific dynamics of each location.

Therefore, before delving into the exploration of the real estate market and the intricate details of property acquisition, take a moment to recognize the wealth of global diversity you are venturing into. Every nation has its own rules and customs rooted in its history and culture.

This preface is a call to caution and cultural sensitivity. May it serve as a beacon that lights the way, reminding you that, in the pursuit of your home, you are immersing yourself in a unique experience shaped by both the laws and customs ingrained in the land you choose to call your own.

May this guide be your compass on this journey, guiding you through the unique waters of property acquisition in diverse lands. Welcome to an adventure that will transform your life and take you across borders and boundaries toward the realization of your real estate dreams!

Content

1. Introduction
a. Purpose of the guide
b. Importance of real estate investment

2. Personal finances
a. Assessment of financial capacity
b. Budgeting and financing
c. Credit score review

3. Market research
a. Local real estate market trends
b. Average property prices
c. Future developments in the area

4. Define search criteria
a. Type of property (house, apartment, land)
b. Preferred location
c. Essential features (number of rooms, bathrooms, etc.)

5. Selection of a real estate agent
a. Importance of an agent
b. How to find a reliable agent
c. Key questions to ask the agent

6. Financing process
a. Types of mortgage loans
b. Obtaining pre-approval
c. Required documentation

7. Inspections and evaluations

a. Importance of inspections
b. Types of necessary inspections
c. Property condition assessment

8. Negotiation
a. Negotiation strategies
b. Conditions to consider
c. Legal and financial aspects of the offer

9. Transaction closing
a. Legal process and documents
b. Closing costs
c. Property delivery and transfer

10. Maintenance and improvements
a. Maintenance planning
b. Improvement projects
c. Homeowner's insurance

11. Additional resources
a. Legal and financial guides
b. Online tools for property search
c. Local real estate organizations

12. Final tips
a. Flexibility in the search
b. Taking the necessary time
c. Consulting with professionals when needed

13. Frequently Asked Questions
a. Addressing common buyer questions
b. Providing additional information on common concerns

Introduction

Purpose of the Guide

The purpose of this comprehensive guide for property buyers is to provide a thorough and accessible reference that enables potential real estate buyers to navigate with confidence through the complex process of property acquisition. From the initial assessment of financial capability to the signing of closing documents, this guide aims to equip buyers with the necessary knowledge to make informed and strategic decisions at every stage of the real estate process.

Through detailed information on financial aspects, market research, selection of real estate agents, negotiation, inspections, evaluations, and transaction closing, we aspire to empower buyers, providing them with essential tools to maximize their investments and avoid potential obstacles.

This guide not only focuses on the practical aspects of property buying but also covers topics related to maintenance, improvements, and legal aspects, ensuring that buyers are fully prepared to take on the responsibility of property ownership effectively and successfully.

Our intention is to be the comprehensive resource that buyers can turn to in their search for a property, guiding them from the initial planning stages to the possibility of becoming homeowners or successful investors in the real estate market.

Importance of Real Estate Investment

Real estate investment plays a fundamental role in building long-term wealth and financial security. Its significance extends beyond the mere acquisition of properties and is highlighted by several key aspects. Below are some crucial reasons that underscore the importance of real estate investment:

Equity Growth: Over time, properties tend to increase in value, providing investors with the opportunity to accumulate significant equity. This growth can be particularly beneficial in areas of ongoing development and sustained growth.

Generation of Passive Income: Real estate properties can provide stable income streams through rentals. This source of passive income is crucial for diversifying income sources and ensuring long-term financial stability.

Protection against Inflation: Real estate properties tend to retain their value during inflationary periods. As prices rise, property values and rental income also tend to adjust accordingly.

Portfolio Diversification: Real estate investment offers a tangible and diversified way to invest, complementing traditional investments in stocks and bonds. Diversifying the portfolio reduces overall risk and provides a balanced strategy for financial growth.

Tax Benefits: Real estate investors often can take advantage of tax benefits, such as mortgage interest deductions, depreciation, and property-related expenses. These incentives can significantly contribute to the profitability of the investment.

Inheritance and Wealth Transfer: Real estate can serve as an efficient vehicle for transferring wealth to future generations. In addition to providing valuable assets, it can also offer financial stability to subsequent generations.

Long-Term Stability: Unlike more volatile investment types, the real estate market tends to be more stable over the long term. This provides investors with greater security and predictability compared to other forms of investment.

In summary, real estate investment not only offers opportunities for capital growth and income generation but also provides a solid foundation for wealth building and long-term financial planning. Its importance lies in its ability to deliver tangible and sustainable benefits over time.

Personal Finance

The evaluation of financial capacity is an essential step in the property purchasing process, allowing individuals to realistically assess their ability to handle real estate investment. This process involves a thorough review of available financial resources and an understanding of the financial obligations associated with acquiring a property. The key elements of financial capacity assessment are highlighted below:

Stable Income: Analyzing and quantifying stable income is crucial. This includes salaries, additional income, investments, and any other regular sources of income. The stability of these earnings provides a solid foundation for assessing the ability to meet mortgage payments and other associated expenses.

Debts and Financial Obligations: Identifying and quantifying existing debts, such as student loans, credit cards, or car loans, is essential. Understanding the monthly obligations associated with these debts allows for the calculation of additional borrowing capacity for a mortgage.

Credit History: Reviewing the credit history is crucial for gaining a clear insight into financial strength. A good credit history facilitates obtaining favorable interest rates and more advantageous loan terms.

Monthly Expenses and Budget: Evaluating monthly expenses, including utilities, insurance, transportation, and other recurring costs, is essential for determining the ability to sustain additional property-related costs. Creating a detailed budget helps visualize the financial impact of the investment.

Down Payment and Closing Costs: Considering the availability of funds for the down payment and closing costs is crucial. These initial costs are essential for completing the transaction and should be an integral part of the financial assessment.

Emergency Fund: Maintaining an emergency fund is crucial to address unexpected expenses. This reserve can act as a financial cushion for unforeseen situations, ensuring long-term financial stability.

Debt-to-Income Ratio (DTI): Calculating the debt-to-income ratio, which compares debt payments to monthly income, provides a clear indication of the ability to take on new debts, such as a mortgage.

Career and Life Expectations: Considering career prospects and changes in personal life that may impact long-term financial stability. Evaluating how real estate investment aligns with future goals and plans.

By conducting a comprehensive assessment of financial capacity, buyers can make informed decisions about the affordability of a property and ensure a solid and financially sustainable home-buying experience.

Financial capacity assessment

Financial Capacity Assessment is a crucial and thoughtful step that property buyers should undertake before embarking on the home acquisition process. This process involves a detailed analysis of personal financial situations to determine the strength and sustainability of the real estate investment. The fundamental aspects covered in the financial capacity assessment are outlined below:

Income and Financial Stability: Carefully examine regular income from sources such as salaries, additional income, or investments. Assess the stability of these incomes over time to anticipate the ability to meet long-term financial commitments.

Debts and Previous Financial Commitments: Identify and quantify existing debts, including student loans, credit cards, and other financial obligations. Analyze the ability to manage new financial obligations based on existing debts.

Credit History: Thoroughly review the credit history to understand financial health and the ability to access favorable interest rates in mortgage loans.

Monthly Budget: Develop a detailed budget that includes all monthly expenses, from utilities to maintenance costs and insurance. Evaluate the ability to adjust the budget to accommodate additional costs associated with property ownership.

Initial Costs: Consider the availability of funds for the down payment and closing costs, ensuring a smooth real estate transaction.

Emergency Reserve: Maintain a financial reserve to address potential unforeseen events, such as unexpected repairs or temporary loss of income.

Debt-to-Income Ratio (DTI): Calculate the debt-to-income ratio to understand how debt payments, including the proposed mortgage, align with monthly income.

Career and Life Outlook: Consider career expectations and possible changes in personal life that may impact long-term financial stability.

Conducting a comprehensive financial capacity assessment provides a solid foundation for making informed decisions, ensuring that the real estate investment is a financially viable and sustainable long-term endeavor.

Budget and Financing

The property acquisition process begins with careful budget planning and consideration of available financing options. These elements are crucial to ensure a successful and financially viable transaction. The essential aspects of Budget and Financing are detailed below:

Budget Development: Start with a detailed analysis of monthly income and regular expenses. Identify areas where the budget can be adjusted to accommodate costs associated with property purchase.

Costs Associated with Purchase: Recognize and anticipate various initial costs, such as the down payment, closing costs, appraisals, and potential repairs. Include these costs in the budget to avoid financial surprises.

Assessing Borrowing Capacity: Consider the debt-to-income ratio (DTI) to understand how much of monthly income is allocated to debt payments. Determine how much can realistically be allocated to mortgage payments without compromising financial stability.

Financing Options: Explore different mortgage loan options, including fixed and adjustable rates, terms, and special programs. Compare interest rates and conditions to select the option that best fits needs and financial capacity.

Obtaining Pre-approval: Seek mortgage pre-approval to have a clear understanding of the amount that can be requested and instill confidence in sellers during the negotiation process.

Consider Incentives and Government Programs: Research potential tax incentives and government programs that can facilitate home buying, such as government-backed loans or down payment assistance programs.

Maintaining an Emergency Reserve: Ensure the existence of a financial reserve that can cover possible unexpected expenses during and after the purchase process.

Professional Advice: Consult with financial advisors and mortgage experts for personalized guidance and to make informed decisions.

A careful approach to budget planning and the appropriate selection of financing options are essential elements to ensure a property buying experience that is financially sound and satisfying in the long term.

Credit Score Review

The credit score review is a critical step in preparing for property acquisition, as the state of our credit history can significantly influence the ability to secure favorable financing. The essential aspects of the "Credit Score Review" are outlined below:

Obtaining Credit Reports: Requesting copies of credit reports from relevant agencies such as Equifax, Experian, and TransUnion.
Thoroughly reviewing the information to ensure its accuracy and timeliness.

Understanding Credit Score Components: Familiarizing oneself with factors influencing the credit score, such as payment history, credit utilization, credit history, types of credit, and recent inquiries.

Error Correction: Identifying and disputing any errors or discrepancies in credit reports.
Ensuring that negative, incorrect, or outdated information is corrected to accurately reflect the financial situation.

Establishing Solid Payment Habits: Ensuring timely fulfillment of all payment obligations, such as credit cards and loans.
Avoiding late payments or defaults, as these can negatively impact the credit score.

Debt Reduction: Working on reducing credit card balances and other loans to improve the debt-to-income ratio and credit utilization.
Avoiding accumulating excessive balances compared to available credit limits.

Loan Application Planning: Being strategic in applying for new credits and loans before property hunting. Avoiding multiple credit inquiries in a short period, as this can temporarily affect the credit score.

Responsible Credit Usage: Maintaining a healthy balance between different types of credit, such as credit cards, auto loans, and mortgages.
Demonstrating a strong and diverse credit history.

Professional Guidance: Consulting with financial advisors or credit specialists for specific and strategic guidance to improve the credit score.

Diligent review and strengthening of the credit score are fundamental steps to securing the most favorable financing conditions when embarking on the property purchase process. A good credit score not only facilitates mortgage loan approval but can also result in lower interest rates and more advantageous terms.

Market Research

Market research is an essential component for understanding the dynamics and trends that guide business decision-making. Several methodological steps must be followed to obtain a comprehensive and accurate view of the business environment. The key aspects of effective market research are detailed below.

Digitalization and Technology: Digitalization has left a significant mark on the real estate market. Online platforms, virtual reality, and data analysis tools are changing how buyers search for properties and how real estate agents manage their businesses.

Sustainability and Energy Efficiency: With growing environmental awareness, the demand for sustainable and energy-efficient properties is on the rise. Buyers are seeking buildings that minimize their environmental impact and offer eco-friendly solutions.

Workspace Flexibility: The trend towards remote work has impacted real estate preferences. There is an increase in demand for properties that provide suitable spaces for remote work, as well as proximity to coworking areas.

Rising Peripheral Locations: Urbanization continues, but people are also exploring opportunities in peripheral areas. Accessibility, quality of life, and more affordable prices are driving interest in locations outside metropolitan areas.

Multifunctional Properties: Versatility in space usage is key. Buyers are looking for properties that adapt to various needs, whether for living, working, or investing. This has boosted interest in real estate developments that offer a combination of residential and commercial spaces.

Digital Real Estate Investments: Digital real estate investment platforms allow investors to participate in the market with lower amounts and greater liquidity. This democratized approach is gaining popularity, especially among younger investors.

Regulations and Government Policies: Changes in government policies and regulations can have a significant impact on the real estate market. Whether through tax incentives, zoning restrictions, or housing programs, government decisions influence market dynamics.

Innovation in Financing: New forms of financing, such as digital mortgages and blockchain-based models, are transforming the property acquisition process. These innovations aim to make the process more efficient and accessible.

In summary, the local real estate market is undergoing an evolution marked by technology, sustainability, and adaptability to changing consumer needs. Those who are attentive to these trends will be better positioned to seize emerging opportunities in this dynamic sector.

Average Property Prices: Average property prices are a key indicator in the real estate market, reflecting the economic health and dynamics of a specific geographical area. Currently, various factors influence the determination of these prices, creating a complex yet revealing landscape. The following are some relevant aspects related to average property prices:

Location: Location remains a determining factor in property prices. Well-connected urban areas with nearby services and good infrastructure tend to have higher prices compared to peripheral areas.

Supply and Demand: The basic law of supply and demand significantly influences property prices. In areas where demand exceeds supply, prices tend to increase, and vice versa.

Economic Cycles: Regional and national economic cycles also play a crucial role. During periods of economic growth, property prices usually experience an increase, while in recessions, they may stabilize or even decrease.

Property Features:

Factors such as size, construction quality, amenities, and the age of the property directly impact its value. Well-maintained properties with attractive features generally command higher prices.

Real Estate Development: The presence of new real estate developments can influence the prices of surrounding properties. The perception of a growing area can increase demand and, consequently, prices.

Market Trends: Current market trends, such as digitization, sustainability, and the demand for flexible spaces, can also affect property prices. Properties aligning with these trends often have added value.

Financing Conditions: Interest rates and financing terms play a crucial role. Low-interest rates can incentivize investment and increase demand, positively affecting prices.

Government Regulations: Changes in government policies, such as tax incentives or zoning restrictions, can have a direct impact on property prices.

Impact of External Events: External events, such as global economic crises or pandemics, can have significant consequences on property prices, leading to unforeseen fluctuations.

Appraisal History: Analyzing the appraisal history of properties in a specific area provides a long-term perspective on how prices have evolved, allowing for more informed projections.

In conclusion, average property prices result from a complex interplay of various factors. Understanding these elements is essential for making informed decisions in the real estate domain.

Future Developments in the Area

Future developments in a particular area are crucial elements for anticipating the evolution of the environment and making strategic decisions. In this context, several factors suggest possible directions for growth and transformation in the near future.

Urban Innovation: The implementation of urban innovation projects, such as smart areas, sustainable mobility, and digitization of services, could redefine the infrastructure and quality of life in the area. The adoption of emerging technologies will contribute to creating more efficient and connected urban environments.

Commercial and Business Development: Attracting commercial and business investments can drive economic development in the area. Establishing business centers, industrial parks, or areas dedicated to innovation and technology may generate employment and foster economic growth.

Sustainable Residential Projects: Growing environmental awareness is leading to more sustainable residential developments. Projects incorporating eco-friendly practices, such as energy efficiency and the use of green technologies, could gain prominence and attract environmentally conscious buyers.

Coworking and Collaborative Spaces: The trend towards flexible work models could stimulate the emergence of coworking and collaborative spaces. This not only encourages the creation of business communities but may also influence urban planning and local business dynamics.

Tourism Development: If the area has tourist attractions, additional tourism developments are likely to become a priority. Improving tourism infrastructure, diversifying offerings, and promoting local events could enhance tourist activity.

Transportation Infrastructure Improvements: Projects that enhance accessibility and connectivity, such as expanding public transportation networks, building new roads, or even implementing innovative mobility systems, can redefine mobility in the area and increase its appeal.

Urban Area Rehabilitation: Revitalizing old or degraded urban areas can be a key focus for driving development. Converting abandoned spaces into residential, commercial, or cultural zones can have a significant impact on the revitalization of the area.

Focus on Green Spaces and Recreation: The creation of parks, trails, and recreational green spaces is a growing trend. Urban planning focused on quality of life, with an emphasis on green areas, can attract residents and promote a healthy lifestyle.

Cultural and Entertainment Projects: Developments that foster culture and entertainment, such as theaters, art galleries, or cultural centers, can contribute to the vitality and diversification of the area, attracting residents and visitors.

Social Development Initiatives: Projects addressing social needs, such as affordable housing, educational facilities, and health centers, may be essential for sustainable and equitable growth in the area.

In summary, future developments in an area can encompass a variety of aspects, from infrastructure to social and economic innovation. Being attentive to these trends provides valuable insights for those making strategic decisions in the realm of local development.

Defining Search Criteria

Defining search criteria is a fundamental step to optimize efficiency and accuracy when seeking information, products, or services. These criteria act as filters that help refine and focus the search according to specific needs. Here are some key aspects to effectively define search criteria.

Property Type (House, Apartment, Land):
The type of property is a crucial element when searching or evaluating real estate. Each property type has distinctive features that align with different preferences and needs. The attributes of the most common property types – house, apartment, and land – are briefly described below:

House: Houses are standalone structures that generally offer greater privacy and space. Their design can vary from single-family homes to townhouses. Houses often include surrounding land and provide homeowners with the opportunity to customize both the interior and exterior according to their preferences. This property type is ideal for those who value autonomy and desire a more spacious living space.

Apartment: Apartments, also known as flats, are housing units within shared buildings. They offer a more compact option and are suitable for those seeking more centralized amenities. Apartments are often located in urban areas and may include shared services such as common areas, security, and parking.

This property type is popular among those looking for a practical and low-maintenance option.

Land: Land is simply undeveloped space, such as an empty lot or plot of land, offering the possibility of building a property according to the owner's preferences. Purchasing land is an attractive option for those wanting to build a custom home or for investors seeking future development. Choosing land provides flexibility and control over design and construction.

Each property type has its own advantages and considerations, and the choice will largely depend on the individual buyer's or investor's needs and goals. While houses offer autonomy and space, apartments provide shared amenities and a more compact option. On the other hand, land purchase offers the opportunity to build from scratch. The final decision will depend on factors such as lifestyle, personal preferences, location, and budget.

Preferred Location

The choice of a preferred location is a crucial aspect when selecting a property or establishing a new place of residence. The location not only impacts lifestyle but also influences access to services, safety, and long-term investment. Below are some factors that could influence the choice of a preferred location:

Accessibility: Proximity to key transportation routes, such as major roads, public transportation, and airports, can be essential. An accessible location facilitates daily commutes and improves connectivity with other areas.

Services and Amenities: The availability of essential services such as schools, hospitals, shopping centers, and parks can make a location more attractive. The convenience of having these services nearby can significantly enhance the quality of life.

Security: Security is a crucial factor. Preference for areas with low crime rates and effective security measures can influence location choice, especially for those seeking a residential environment.

Natural Environment: The presence of natural environments, such as parks, green areas, or proximity to water, can be a significant draw. These elements contribute to environmental quality and overall well-being.

Development Prospects: Evaluating future development prospects in the area can be crucial. An area experiencing economic growth may offer long-term investment opportunities and potential increases in property value.

Climate and Geography: Personal preferences for climate and geography also play a role. Some individuals may prefer warm climates, while others seek cooler environments or specific geographical features such as mountains or beaches.

Culture and Lifestyle: Affinity with the local culture and community lifestyle can be a determining factor. Some may seek vibrant and culturally rich areas, while others prefer quieter and more traditional environments.

Cost of Living: Assessing the cost of living in a specific location is crucial to ensure it aligns with the budget. This includes not only housing prices but also daily expenses and local taxes.

Job Opportunities: Proximity to job opportunities and business centers can be a key factor, especially for those looking to minimize commute times and capitalize on local professional opportunities.

Choosing a preferred location involves a balance of multiple factors, and the final decision will largely depend on individual priorities and goals. Considering these aspects provides a solid foundation for making informed decisions and finding a location that best suits personal and family needs.

Essential Features (Number of Rooms, Bathrooms, etc.)

The essential features of a property play a crucial role in evaluating housing options. These elements are determinants of the comfort and functionality of the living space. Here are some of the essential features typically considered by buyers or tenants when looking for a property:

Number of Rooms: The number of rooms is one of the most crucial aspects. This factor is directly related to the ability to accommodate residents comfortably and provide flexibility for specific needs, such as guest rooms or workspace.

Number of Bathrooms: The number of bathrooms is another key element. Adequate bathroom distribution can enhance daily comfort and prevent congestion, especially in homes with multiple residents.

Kitchen Size: The kitchen is the heart of the home. Spacious and functional kitchens facilitate food preparation and allow for the incorporation of dining areas, turning the kitchen into a central hub for socializing.

Storage Areas: Storage spaces, such as built-in closets and additional areas for storing items, are fundamental. These contribute to maintaining order and organization in the home.

Space Distribution and Design: The distribution and design of space impact the functionality and aesthetics of the home. Well-planned design can maximize space utilization and create a cozy atmosphere.

Laundry Facilities: The presence of laundry facilities, either within the home or in a common area of the building, is essential for daily convenience. It facilitates household chores and eliminates the need to travel to external facilities.

Parking and Garage: The availability of parking, whether on the street, assigned parking, or a garage, is an important factor, especially in urban areas or spaces with limited parking.

Community Amenities and Services: The presence of community amenities and services, such as pools, gyms, recreational areas, or 24-hour security, can enhance the quality of life and the perceived value of the property.

Energy Efficiency and Technology: Modern features, such as energy efficiency and smart technologies, may be essential considerations. These features not only contribute to energy savings but also enhance the overall living experience.

Maintenance Condition and Recent Renovations: The overall condition of the property and any recent renovations are aspects to consider. A well-maintained and updated home provides greater comfort and may reduce the need for short-term repairs.

Considering these essential features allows buyers or tenants to make informed decisions when selecting a property that fits their individual needs and preferences.

Selecting a Real Estate Agent

The importance of a real estate agent lies in their ability to facilitate and optimize the process of buying or selling properties. Their expertise and specialized knowledge add significant value to various stages of the real estate transaction. Here are some key reasons to consider the importance of a real estate agent:

Market Knowledge: Real estate agents have a deep understanding of the local market. This includes knowledge of trends, comparable property prices, and market dynamics in the specific area, which is invaluable when devising buying or selling strategies.

Network and Resources: An agent's network can open doors to opportunities that might be challenging to access otherwise. They have connections with other real estate professionals, such as lawyers, appraisers, and lenders, who can facilitate the process.

Negotiation Skills: Negotiation skills are crucial in the real estate realm. An experienced agent can effectively represent your interests, negotiate prices and conditions, and secure deals that are advantageous to you.

Access to Exclusive Properties: Real estate agents often have access to exclusive properties not available to the general public. This expands the available options and can lead to the identification of unique opportunities.

Document Handling and Procedures: Buying or selling properties involves a significant amount of documentation and legal procedures. An agent can efficiently handle this paperwork, ensuring that all legal aspects are in order and avoiding potential complications.

Market Value Assessment: Real estate agents have the ability to accurately assess the market value of a property. This ensures that, whether you are buying or selling, you are involved in fair and equitable transactions.

Professional Advice: A real estate agent can provide professional advice based on their experience. They can help you understand financial implications, assess risks, and make informed decisions at each stage of the process.

Time and Effort Savings: Involving a real estate agent simplifies the process for you. They coordinate visits, handle negotiations, conduct market research, and take care of multiple tasks, allowing you to save time and effort.

Adaptation to Market Changes: Agents are aware of market changes and can adjust strategies accordingly. Their ability to adapt to changing conditions can be crucial for the success of the transaction.

Transparency and Professional Ethics: An ethical real estate agent provides transparency and honesty at all stages of the transaction. This builds trust and ensures that you are well-represented in the process.

In summary, the importance of a real estate agent lies in their ability to simplify, optimize, and ensure a successful transaction. Their experience and resources provide valuable support, allowing you to make more informed decisions and efficiently achieve your real estate goals.

How to Find a Reliable Real Estate Agent

Finding a reliable real estate agent is crucial to ensuring a positive and successful experience in the process of buying or selling a property. Here are some fundamental steps to identify and select a trustworthy agent.

Online Research: Start your search online. Explore real estate websites, review platforms, and professional profiles of agents. Examine reviews and feedback from previous clients to get an idea of the agent's reputation.

Personal Recommendations: Ask family, friends, or colleagues who have had positive experiences with real estate agents. Personal recommendations are a valuable source of information and can provide unique perspectives.

Credential Verification: Ensure that the agent is properly licensed and has the necessary credentials. You can verify this through the local real estate regulatory agency. Membership in professional associations can also be an indicator of commitment and ethics.

Market Experience: Give preference to agents with significant experience in the local market. A deep understanding of local trends, property prices, and market dynamics is essential for making informed decisions.

Personal Interviews: Schedule personal interviews with potential agents. This is an opportunity to assess their level of professionalism, communication, and ability to understand your specific needs. Inquire about their previous experience and success stories.

Portfolio of Previous Properties: Request to see the portfolio of properties the agent has handled in the past. This will give you an idea of their experience and the variety of transactions they have completed.

Connections and Network: Evaluate the agent's network of contacts. A broad network can be an indicator of their ability to facilitate transactions and connect you with key professionals in the process, such as appraisers and lawyers.

Communication Style: Observe the agent's communication style. Clear and proactive communication is essential in real estate transactions. Ensure that the agent is willing to keep you informed at every stage of the process.

Marketing Strategies: If you are selling a property, evaluate the agent's marketing strategies. Ask them how they plan to promote your property and reach potential buyers.

Transparency about Costs and Fees: Ensure that you clearly understand the cost and fee structure of the agent. A reliable agent will provide transparent information about the costs associated with their services.

By following these steps, you will be better equipped to find a reliable real estate agent that fits your needs and goals. Transparency, experience, and professional ethics are key elements to consider to ensure a successful collaboration with your real estate agent.

Key Questions to Ask the Real Estate Agent

When interacting with a real estate agent, asking key questions is essential to gather relevant information and make informed decisions. Here are some key questions you may consider asking the real estate agent:

Professional Experience: How long have you been working as a real estate agent?
What is your specific experience in the local market?

References and Testimonials: Can you provide references from previous clients?
Do you have online testimonials or reviews that I can review?

Knowledge of the Local Market: How would you describe the current market trends in this area?
How many transactions have you recently completed in this neighborhood?

Marketing Strategies (if selling): What is your marketing approach for selling properties?
How do you plan to effectively promote my property?

Average Time on the Market: How long do properties typically stay on the market with your clients?
Do you have specific strategies to expedite the selling process?

Communication and Availability: What is your preferred method of communication, and how often can I expect updates?
Are you available to show properties or discuss details outside regular business hours?

Negotiation and Buying/Selling Strategies: What is your approach to negotiations?
Have you faced challenging situations in the past, and how did you handle them?

Network of Contacts and Resources: Do you have a strong network of contacts that can benefit the transaction?
Do you work with professionals such as appraisers, lawyers, or trusted home inspectors?

Costs and Fees: What is your fee structure, and how are associated costs handled?
Are there additional fees that I should be aware of?

Short and Long-Term Market Outlook: What are your perspectives on the real estate market in the short and long term?
Are there economic or developmental factors that may impact investment in this area?

Exclusivity and Representation Agreement: Are you willing to work exclusively with me during this process?
How does the representation agreement work, and what are its terms?

These questions will help you assess the suitability of the real estate agent for your needs and gain a better understanding of their approach and skills. Open communication and transparency are key to establishing an effective collaboration with your real estate agent.

Additional Resources

The Additional Resources section is crucial for property buyers as it provides access to valuable information and support throughout the entire purchasing process. Here are detailed resources and tools that complement the guide and enhance the buyer's experience:

Legal and Financial Guides: Recommendations for books, documents, and online guides addressing legal and financial aspects related to property purchases. Educational material that clarifies legal terms, contractual processes, and key financial concepts.

Online Tools for Property Search: Online real estate platforms that facilitate property search and comparison. Applications and websites providing detailed market information, price trends, and specific neighborhood data.

Local Real Estate Organizations: Contacts and links to local real estate organizations that offer advice, events, and resources specific to the community. Involvement in local real estate networks to gather information on local market opportunities and challenges.

Real Estate Seminars and Webinars: Announcements of seminars and webinars covering relevant topics such as investment strategies, financing tips, and market changes. Resources offering the opportunity to learn from real estate experts and industry professionals.

Financial Calculators: Links to online calculators that help buyers estimate mortgage payments, closing costs, and other related expenses. Tools that allow for financial simulations to assess different scenarios and loan options.

Online Forums and Communities: Participation in online forums and communities where buyers share experiences, tips, and resources. Discussion platforms that provide the opportunity to ask questions and get answers from individuals who have gone through the purchasing process.

Legal and Mortgage Advisory Services: References to industry professionals, such as real estate attorneys and mortgage advisors. Information on how to select and work with professionals providing specialized guidance.

Information on Incentives and Government Programs: Resources detailing government programs and tax benefits available to property buyers. Updates on changes in government policies that may impact real estate investment.

By providing these additional resources, buyers are offered valuable support to make informed decisions and access up-to-date and relevant information throughout the entire property purchasing process.

Final Tips

Final Tips serve as the culmination of the property buyer's guide, offering key guidance to successfully conclude the acquisition process. Here are final tips aimed at enhancing the buyer's experience:

Flexibility in Search: Keep an open mind and be flexible in your search criteria. The perfect property may not meet all requirements, but it could be an excellent investment.

Take the Necessary Time: Purchasing a property is a significant decision. Take the time to research, plan, and consider all options before committing.

Thorough Inspection: Conduct detailed inspections. Do not skimp on investigating the property's condition to avoid unpleasant surprises after the purchase.

Consult with Professionals: Do not hesitate to seek guidance from professionals. Real estate agents, specialized attorneys, and financial advisors can offer valuable insights and ensure a successful transaction.

Strategic Negotiation: Develop strategic negotiation skills. Understand when to compromise and when to hold your position to secure the best possible terms.

Consider Legal and Financial Aspects: Familiarize yourself with the specific legal and financial aspects of the transaction in your area. Solid knowledge will protect you during the purchase process.

Neighborhood Evaluation: Thoroughly research the neighborhood. Factors such as safety, local services, and future development can significantly impact the value of your investment.

Final Document Review: Before signing, carefully review all legal and financial documents. Make sure you fully understand the terms and conditions of the transaction.

Budget for Additional Costs: Account for potential additional costs. In addition to the mortgage, consider taxes, insurance, maintenance, and planned improvements.

Maintenance Planning: Develop a plan for ongoing property maintenance. Schedule regular inspections and address issues before they become costly situations.

Homeowner's Insurance: Obtain appropriate homeowner's insurance. Protect your investment against risks such as fires, floods, and other adverse events.

Utilize Resources for Investment: If the purchase is for investment purposes, leverage additional resources, such as property management, to maximize return on investment.

By incorporating these final tips into your approach to property purchase, you will be better prepared to tackle challenges and seize opportunities that this process entails. Patience, diligence, and informed decision-making are key to ensuring success in your new real estate investment.

Frequently Asked Questions about Property Purchase

What is the first step in buying a property? Begin with an assessment of your financial capacity. Obtain a mortgage pre-approval to understand how much you can afford to spend.

How much should I allocate for a down payment? A down payment of 20% of the purchase price is recommended, but options with lower down payments are also available.

How do I select a reliable real estate agent? Research, read reviews, and interview multiple agents. Choose someone with experience in the local market who understands your needs.

What should I consider when choosing the property location? Evaluate accessibility, local services, safety, and area growth prospects. Location impacts the long-term value of the property.

How important is the credit history in obtaining a mortgage loan? A good credit history facilitates approval and can result in lower interest rates. Review and improve your credit before applying for a loan.

How can I assess the condition of a property during an inspection? Hire a professional inspector. Ensure you review key elements such as structure, plumbing, electricity, and HVAC systems.

What additional costs should I consider besides the purchase price? Consider closing costs, taxes, insurance, maintenance, and potential improvements. A comprehensive budget is essential.

Is a lawyer necessary for property purchase? While not mandatory, having a real estate attorney can provide crucial legal advice and ensure a smooth transaction.

How can I ensure I get the best deal during negotiation? Research the market, understand price trends, and work with your agent to formulate a competitive offer. Be flexible but also firm in your limits.

When is the right time to buy a property? The right time varies based on personal circumstances and market conditions. Pay attention to interest rates and economic stability.

Is it advisable to buy a property as an investment? It can be a solid strategy. Research the market, calculate return on investment, and consider factors such as location and growth potential.

How long does it take to close a purchase transaction? The time can vary, but the process typically takes 30 to 45 days from accepted offer to closing. Factors like financing and inspections can affect the duration.

These answers provide a general overview, but it's crucial to seek personalized advice and qualified professionals to address your specific needs during the property purchase process.

Buyer's Checklist

Before embarking on the exciting adventure of purchasing a property, it is essential to follow a detailed checklist to ensure a seamless experience. Here is a step-by-step guide:

Financial Capacity Assessment:

Review your credit score and correct any potential errors.
Calculate the debt-to-income ratio (DTI) to understand your borrowing capacity.
Obtain a mortgage pre-approval to establish a realistic price range.

Definition of Search Criteria:

Determine the type of property you are looking for (house, apartment, land).
Specify your preferences regarding location, number of bedrooms, amenities, etc.
Set your budget limits.

Selection of a Real Estate Agent:

Research and interview multiple real estate agents.
Verify the agent's experience in the local market.
Confirm that the agent has a solid reputation and good reviews.

Market Research:

Analyze local real estate market trends.
Compare prices of similar properties in the area.
Research future developments that may affect the property's value.

Financing Process:
Explore different mortgage loan options.
Compare interest rates and loan terms.
Gather the necessary documentation for the loan application.

Inspections and Evaluations:
Schedule professional property inspections.
Evaluate the need for specific inspections (structural, electrical, plumbing, etc.).
Review inspection reports and address any identified issues.

Negotiation:
Develop a negotiation strategy with your agent.
Set clear limits and priorities in your negotiations.
Consider market conditions when formulating your offer.

Transaction Closing:
Review all legal and financial documents before signing.
Ensure you understand closing costs and make necessary payments.
Confirm the effective transfer of the property.

Maintenance and Improvements:
Develop a plan for regular maintenance.
Consider improvement projects based on your needs and budget.

Acquire appropriate homeowner's insurance.

Additional Resources:

Explore online resources and literature related to
property and real estate investment.
Participate in local real estate seminars or events.
Consult with professionals for additional advice as
needed.

This checklist provides a solid framework to guide your
property purchase process. Make sure to customize it
according to your specific needs and seek guidance
from qualified professionals along the way.

References and Useful Links

Here are references and useful links that complement the property buyer's guide, providing additional information and valuable resources to facilitate your experience:

Financing and Credit:
AnnualCreditReport.com: Request free credit reports from the three major credit bureaus.
Bankrate - Financial Calculators: Tools to estimate mortgage payments and other financial calculations.

Property Search:
Realtor.com: Real estate platform for searching properties for sale.
Zillow: Provides property listings, value estimates, and advanced search tools.

Legal and Mortgage Counseling:
FindLaw - Real Estate Attorneys: Legal resources related to real estate.
HUD.gov - Mortgage Counseling: Information on government-backed mortgage counseling programs.

Real Estate Organizations and Networks:

National Association of Realtors (NAR): National association of real estate agents, offering resources and statistics.
BiggerPockets: Online community for real estate investors, with forums and educational resources.

Government Programs and Tax Benefits:

HUD.gov - Housing Programs: Information on government-backed housing programs.
IRS - Real Estate Deductions: IRS page on real estate-related tax deductions.

Neighborhood Research Tools:
NeighborhoodScout: Provides detailed data on neighborhoods, crime rates, and schools.
City-Data.com: Offers demographic, educational, and housing statistics by city.

Continuing Education and Events:
Inman News: Real estate news portal and events.
Eventbrite - Real Estate Seminars: Search for local real estate seminars and events.

Government and Regulatory Organizations:
Consumer Financial Protection Bureau (CFPB): Resources for consumers related to financial services, including mortgages.
U.S. Department of Housing and Urban Development (HUD): Information on housing and urban development.

These links and references offer a diverse range of resources to support your property buying process. Remember that information can change, so it's always advisable to verify the currency of resources before using them.

Epilogue

As you reach the end of this property buyer's guide, you've traversed an exciting and challenging path toward acquiring a space you'll soon call home. This journey involves more than just closing transactions and signing documents; it's about understanding the importance of making informed and strategic decisions.

Remember that buying a property is not merely a financial transaction but a fundamental chapter in your life. With each step, you've assessed your financial capabilities, explored the real estate market, negotiated terms and conditions, and ultimately secured a place that aligns with your dreams and goals.

The epilogue of this journey marks the beginning of a new phase. Your home is more than just a property; it's a space where you'll create memories, pursue your objectives, and find refuge in every challenge. As you walk into the future, remember that you've built not just a house but also a connection to stability and personal growth.

This epilogue not only signifies the closure of a chapter but the opening of infinite possibilities. The property you now own is a valuable asset, but it's also a constant reminder of your ability to make informed decisions and achieve significant milestones.

Face the future with confidence, knowing that you've navigated the complex world of real estate with shrewdness and determination. This home is your sanctuary, your haven, and the tangible result of your dedication and effort.

May this epilogue be the prelude to a life filled with happiness, growth, and success in your new home. Onward, courageous homeowner!

Author

Dionisio Melo has carved out a distinguished career through his tireless pursuit of genuinely effective sales strategies for the demanding Latin American market. His influence spans various dimensions of the sales field, exerting a significant impact across the entire region. A graduate of the Universidad Tecnológica de Buenos Aires, he is also a Real Estate Broker and has been a Realtor in the state of Florida, USA, for almost 12 years.

Not confined to being a prominent speaker at sales conferences and an expert guide in training sessions and personal coaching for sellers and agents; he goes above and beyond by sharing his vast experience and innovative sales strategies with a select group of clients.

In addition to his prominent role in the corporate arena, Dionisio Melo has translated his profound knowledge into several books on sales and sales management. Among his most notable works are "220 Responses to Insurance Objections," "The Real Estate

Heart," "100 Responses to Real Estate Objections," and "100 Responses to Objections Raised by Clients to Private Cemetery Advisors." He has also contributed to "Sales Strategies for Advisors and Managers of Private Cemeteries." These publications reflect his commitment to sales excellence and his ability to address the specific challenges of various sectors.

Dionisio's impact as a sales expert is undeniable; his ideas and insights are omnipresent in companies across virtually all sectors. His popularity transcends borders, reaching an audience of over 20,000 people through newsletters throughout Latin America. Furthermore, his influential blog has been widely shared and republished on numerous business and sales-focused websites.

Dionisio Melo continues to play a crucial role as an advisor to steadily growing companies, providing invaluable support for these companies to reach new levels of success in the competitive Latin American market. His dedication and commitment to sales excellence, backed by his valuable publications, solidify his position as an influential and respected figure in the region.